Sp... FOR DUMMIES®

Pocket Edition

**by Jessica Langemeier**

WILEY

Wiley Publishing, Inc.

**Spanish Phrases For Dummies®, Pocket Edition**

Published by
**Wiley Publishing, Inc.**
111 River St.
Hoboken, NJ 07030-5774
www.wiley.com

For general information on our other products and services, please contact our Customer Care Department within the U.S. at 800-762-2974, outside the U.S. at 317-572-3993, or fax 317-572-4002.

For technical support, please visit www.wiley.com/techsupport.

Wiley also publishes its books in a variety of electronic formats. Some content that appears in print may not be available in electronic books.

ISBN: 978-0-470-43575-5

Manufactured in the United States of America

10  9  8  7  6  5  4  3  2  1

WILEY

# Table of Contents

# Introduction

The Spanish language is growing in popularity. Whether you're at home, at work, or on the go, the Spanish language is everywhere. More and more, people need to understand the basics of Spanish just to get along in their day-to-day lives. And with global travel easier than ever — for business road warriors, students studying abroad, and vacationers — understanding Spanish doesn't have to be a chore when you have *Spanish Phrases For Dummies,* Pocket Edition.

## Conventions Used in This Book

To make this book easy to navigate, I've set up some conventions:

- Spanish words are in *italics* to make them stand out.

- Pronunciation guides to Spanish words are in parentheses.

- Accented syllables are in *italics* in the pronunciation guides. For example, arrivederci (good-bye) is represented as ah-rree-vey-*der*-tchy.

 The Tip icon indicates helpful information that aids in your understanding of pronunciation, grammar, and other elements of the language.

**2**

# Pronouncing Spanish

Pronouncing Spanish words is pretty simple, especially because most letters in Spanish have only one sound — unlike English! Here are some other simple rules:

- ✔ Vowels in Spanish are similar to the English short vowel sound — they are pronounced with a more relaxed mouth and make a softer sound. Thus most vowels in the pronunciation guide are followed by an "h" to remind you to keep your mouth relaxed (ah, eh, ih, oh).

- ✔ The letters "b" and "v" sound very similar, almost like the two letters are combined. The sound is not quite a "b" with the lips pursed, nor is it a "v" with the teeth on the lower lip. Thus the pronunciation guide represents a "b" or "v" by the opposite letter.

- ✔ The "ll" sounds nothing like it looks. In some countries, it sounds like a "j", while in others it sounds like a "y". Thus in the pronunciation guide, "jy" represents a mixture of the sounds.

# Where to Go from Here

You've got your minibook copy of *Spanish Phrases For Dummies,* Pocket Edition — now what? This minibook is a reference, so if you need information on adjectives, head to Chapter 2. Or if you're interested in finding out about how to ask for directions, go straight to Chapter 3. Or heck, start with Chapter 1 and read the chapters in order ... you rebel. If you want even more advice on Spanish, from verb conjugations to more vocabulary, check out the full-size version of *Spanish For Dummies* — simply head to your local book seller or go to www.dummies.com!

# Chapter 1

# Welcome to the Basics

●  ●  ●  ●  ●  ●  ●  ●  ●  ●  ●  ●  ●  ●  ●  ●  ●  ●  ●  ●  ●  ●  ●  ●  ●

*T*his chapter starts you off with the basics of introductions, common words and phrases, and finally words and phrases that you just can't live without. Have some fun!

## *Personal Pronouns*

| | | |
|---|---|---|
| I | *Yo* | (yo) |
| You (S/Informal) | *Tú* | (too) |
| You (S/Formal) | *Usted* (abbreviated *Ud.*) | (oo-*sted*) |
| He | *Él* | (ehl) |
| She | *Ella* | (*ay*-jyah) |
| We | *Nosotros* | (noh-*soh*-trohs) |
| You (P) | *Vosotros* (very formal) | (voh-*soh*-trohs) |
| You (P) | *Ustedes* (formal) | (oo-*sted*-ehs) |
| They | *Ellos* (male or mixed group) | (*ay*-jyohs) |
| | *Ellas* (female group) | (*ay*-jyahs) |

*Usted* (oo-*sted*), "you" in the formal variation, is considered polite and can be used when speaking with a new acquaintance, an elder, a person in a high office, or a superior. When you're familiar with someone or are in a light situation, using *tú* (too), the informal "you," is acceptable.

# Formalities

| Mr./Sir | *Señor* | (seh-*nyour*) |
| Mrs./Ms. | *Señora* | (seh-*nyour*-ah) |
| Miss | *Señorita* | (seh-*nyour*-ee-tah) |

Personal pronouns often are omitted when making statements in Spanish. However, when asking a question, the personal pronoun may remain for emphasis.

# Greetings

| Hello or Hi | *Hola* | (*oh*-lah) |
| Good morning | *Buenos días* | (*bway*-nohs *dee*-ahs) |
| Good afternoon | *Buenas tardes* | (*bway*-nohs *tar*-dehs) |
| Good evening | *Buenas noches* | (*bway*-nahs *no*-chehs) |

| How's it going? (Informal) | *¿Cómo te va?* | (*koh*-moh tay vah?) |
| What's going on?; What's happening? | *¿Qué pasa?* | (kay *pah*-sah?) |

When passing by a person you don't know, it's not typical to say *Hola* (*oh*-lah), as you may say "Hi" in the U.S. More often, you greet strangers with a *Buenos días* (*bway*-nohs *dee*-ahs), *Buenas tardes* (*bway*-nohs *tahr*-dehs), or *Buenas noches* (*bway*-nohs *noh*-chehs). You may also say *Buenos* (*bway*-nohs) or *Buenas* (*bway*-nahs) for short.

# Send-offs

| Goodbye | *Adiós* | (ah-dee-*ohs*) |
| Goodbye (Informal) | *Chau* | (chow) |
| See you later. | *Hasta luego.* | (ahs-tah loo-*way*-goh) |
| See you soon. | *Hasta pronto.* | (ahs-tah pron-toh) |
| See you tomorrow. | *Hasta mañana.* | (ahs-tah mahn-yahn-ah) |
| See you on Friday. | *Hasta viernes.* | (ahs-tah vee-*ehr*-nays) |
| Have a good day! | *¡Que tenga un buen día!* | (kay *tayn*-gah oon bwen *dee*-ah) |

**6**

| Good luck! | *¡Buena suerte!* | (*bway*-nah soo-*wehr*-tay) |
| Take care! (S/P) | *¡Cuídate/Cuídense!* | (ku-ee-dah-tay/ ku-ee-dehn-say) |

## Saying and Replying to "How Are You?"

 You may omit a personal pronoun when making a statement, but when you ask a question, you may want to keep the personal pronoun for emphasis.

**Note:** Unless otherwise indicated, the following questions directed to "you" are in the formal variation, *usted* (oo-*sted*).

| How are you? (Informal) | *¿Cómo estás?* | (*koh*-moh ehs-*tahs*) |
| How are you? (S/Formal) | *¿Cómo está usted?* | (*koh*-moh ehs-tah oo-*sted*) |
| How are you? (P) | *¿Cómo están ustedes?* | (*koh*-moh ehs-tahn oo-sted-ehs) |
| I'm fine, thank you. | *Estoy bien, gracias.* | (ehs-toy bee-en, *grah*-see-ahs) |
| I'm very well. | *Estoy muy bien.* | (ehs-toy moo-ee bee-en) |

| How are things with you? | ¿Cómole van las cosas? | (koh-moh lay vahn lahs koh-sahs?) |
| Things are fine. | Están bien. | (ehs-tahn bee-en) |
| Everything is well. | Todo está bien. | (toh-doh ehs-tah bee-en) |
| I'm okay. | Estoy más o menos. | (ehs-toy mahs oh may-nohs) |
| How is the family? | ¿Cómo está la familia? | (koh-moh ehs-tah lah fah-meel-ee-ah) |
| They're doing well. | Están bien. | (ehs-tahn bee-en) |
| And you? (Informal) | ¿Y tú? | (ee too?) |
| And you? (Formal) | ¿Y usted? | (ee oo-sted?) |
| The same. | Igual. | (ee-gwal) |

# Introducing Yourself and Talking about Where You're From

Unless otherwise indicated, the following questions directed to "you" are in the formal variation, *usted* (oo-*sted*). This practice is considered polite and can be

used when speaking with a new acquaintance, an elder,
a person in a high office, or a superior.

| What is your name? (Formal) | *¿Cómo se llama usted?* | (*koh*-moh say *jya*-ma oo-*sted*?) |
| What is your name? (Informal) | *¿Cómo te llamas tú?* | (*koh*-moh tay *jya*-mas too?) |
| My name is Matthew. | *Me llamo Matthew.* | (may *jya*-mo maht-you) |
| I am Julia. | *Soy Julia.* | (soy *hoo*-lee-ah) |
| What is your first name? | *¿Cuál es su nombre?* | (kwal es soo *nohm*-bray?) |
| My name is Eduardo. | *Mi nombre es Eduardo.* | (me *nohm*-bray ehs ed-*wahr*-doh) |
| And your last name? | *¿Y su apellido?* | (ee soo ah-peh-*jyee*-doh?) |
| My last name is Johnson. | *Mi apellido es Johnson.* | (me ah-peh-*jyee*-doe ehs *yohn*-sohn) |
| How do you spell your name? | *¿Cómo se deletrea su nombre?* | (*koh*-moh say day-lay-*tray*-ah soo *nohm*-bray?) |
| How is your name pronounced? | *¿Cómo se pronuncia su nombre?* | (*koh*-moh say pro-*noon*-see-ah soo *nohm*-bray?) |

| | | |
|---|---|---|
| It's nice to meet you. | *Mucho gusto.* | (*mooch*-oh *goose*-toh) |
| It's a pleasure (to meet you). | *Es un placer (conocerle).* | (ehs oon plah-*sehr* kon-oh-*sehr*-lay) |
| Enchanted. (M) | *Encantado.* | (ehn-kahn-*tah*-doh) |
| Enchanted. (F) | *Encantada.* | (ehn-kahn-*tah*-dah) |
| Likewise. | *Igualmente.* | (ee-gwal-*men*-tay) |
| Where are you from? (Informal) | *¿De dónde eres tú?* | (day *don*-day *ehr*-es too?) |
| Where are you from? (Formal) | *¿De dónde es usted?* | (day *don*-day ehs oo-*sted*?) |
| I am from the United States. | *Soy de los Estados Unidos.* | (soy day lohs ehs-*tah*-dohs oo-*nee*-dohs) |
| Where do you come from? | *¿De dónde es usted?* | *(day don-*day ehs oo-*sted?)* |
| What country are you from? | *¿De cuál país es usted?* | (day kwal pie-*ees* ehs oo-*sted*) |
| I come from Mexico. | *Vengo de México.* | (*bayn*-goh day *meh*-hee-koh) |

When you know someone a little better or you're already acquainted, using *tú* (too), the informal "you," is acceptable.

| Where do you live? | *¿Dónde vives?* | (*don*-day *vee*-vehs?) |
| I live in Monterrey. | *Vivo en Monterrey.* | (*vee*- voh ehn mon-tehr-*ray*) |
| What city are you from? | *¿De cuál ciudad eres tú?* | (day *kwal* see-you-*dad ehr*-es too?) |
| I'm from Chicago, Illinois. | *Soy de Chicago, Illinois.* | (soy day she-*kah*-goh, eel-ee-*noy*) |
| Where do you work? | *¿En dónde trabajas?* | (ehn *don*-day trah-*vah*-has?) |
| I work at the bank. | *Trabajo en el banco.* | (trah-*bah*-ha ehn ehl bahn-koh) |
| What do you do? | *¿En qué trabajas tú?* | (ehn *kay* trah-*bah*-has too?) |
| I work with computers. | *Trabajo en los computadores.* | (trah-*bah*-ho ehn lohs kohm-poo-tah-*door*-ays) |
| I work in business. | *Trabajo en los negocios.* | (trah-*vah*-ho ehn lohs nay-*goh*-see-ohs) |

# Indispensable Words

| yes | *sí* | (see) |
| no | *no* | (noh) |

| please | *por favor* | (pohr fah-*vohr*) |
| thank you | *gracias* | (*grah*-see-ahs) |
| you're welcome | *de nada* | (day nah-dah) |
| no problem | *no hay problema* | (noh eye proh-*blehm*-ah) |
| of course | *claro* | (klah-roh) |
| great | *bueno* | (bway-noh) |
| perfect | *perfecto* | (pehr-*fect*-oh) |
| correct | *correcto* | (kohr-*rect*-oh) |
| delicious | *delicioso* | (day-lees-ee-*oh*-soh) |

## *Asking for Help*

| repeat; say again | *repite* | (reh-*pih*-tay) |
| come | *venga* | (*bayn*-gah) |
| go | *vaya* | (*bye-ah*) |
| I need water. | *Necesito agua.* | (neh-seh-*see*-toh ah-gwua) |
| information | *información* | (ehn-four-mah-see-*ohn*) |
| schedule | *horario* | (ohr-*ahr*-ee-oh) |
| emergency | *emergencia* | (ee-mehr-*hen*-see-ah) |
| doctor | *doctor* | (doc-*tohr*) |

| | | |
|---|---|---|
| accident | *accidente* | (ak-see-*den*-tay) |
| help | *ayuda* | (eye-*yoo*-dah) |
| taxi | *taxi* | (*tahx*-ee) |
| bus | *autobús* or *bus* | (ow-toh-*boos* or boos) |
| car | *coche* or *carro* | (*koh*-chay or kahr-roh) |

# Miscellaneous Useful Words

| | | |
|---|---|---|
| to | *a* | (ah) |
| at | *a* | (ah) |
| from | *de* | (day) |
| about | *de* | (day) |
| because | *porque* | (pohr-kay) |
| and | *y* | (ee) |
| or | o | *(oh)* |
| a/an (M/F) | *un/una* | (oon/oon-*ah*) |
| the (M/S) | *el* | (ehl) |
| the (F/S) | *la* | (lah) |
| the (M/P) | *los* | (lohs) |
| the (F/P) | *las* | (lahs) |
| some (M/F) | *unos/unas* | (oo-*nohs*/oo-*nahs*) |

| again | *otra vez* | (*oh*-trah vays) |
| another | *otra/otro* | (*oh*-trah/*oh*-troh) |
| more | *más* | (mahs) |
| better | *mejor* | (may-*hohr*) |
| big | *grande* | (*grahn*-day) |
| small | *chico/pequeño* | (*chee*-koh/ peh-*kay*-nyo) |
| fast | *rápido* | (*rahp*-ee-doh) |
| slow | *lento* | (*lehn*-toh) |
| easy | *fácil* | (*fah*-seel) |
| difficult | *difícil* | (dee-*fee*-seel) |

## *Places*

When you're beginning a new language, or when you're having trouble with nouns, it's best to focus on the main idea and not worry about articles. For that reason, the following list of nouns doesn't include the masculine or feminine forms of "a" (*un* (oon) [M] and *una* (oo-*nah*) [F]) or "the" (*el* (ehl) [M] and *la* (lah) [F]).

| city | *ciudad* | (see-yoo-*dahd*) |
| country | *país* | (pie-*ees*) |
| appointment | *cita* | (*see*-tah) |

| | | |
|---|---|---|
| office | *oficina* | (off-ee-*see*-nah) |
| airport | *aeropuerto* | (ehr-oh-*pwehr*-toh) |
| hospital | *hospital* | (*ohs*-pee-tahl) |
| clinic | *clínica* | (*clee*-nee-kah) |
| restaurant | *restaurante* | (rest-ow-*rahn*-tay) |
| house | *casa* | (kah-sah) |
| hotel | *hotel* | (oh-*tehl*) |
| building | *edificio* | (eh-dee-*fee*-see-oh) |
| bathroom | *baño* | (*bah*-nyo) |

# People

| | | |
|---|---|---|
| people | *gente* | (hen-tay) |
| man | *hombre* | (ohm-bray) |
| woman | *mujer* | (moo-*hehr*) |
| boy (Formal/Informal) | *niño/chico* | (nee-*nyoh*/chee-koh) |
| girl (Formal/Informal) | *niña/chica* | (nee-*nyah*/chee-kah) |
| family | *familia* | (fah-*meel*-ee-ah) |
| wife | *esposa* | (ehs-*poh*-sah) |
| husband | *marido* | (mah-*ree*-doh) |
| mother (Formal/Informal) | *madre/mama* | (*mah*-dray/mah-*mah*) |

| | | |
|---|---|---|
| father (Formal/Informal) | *padre/papa* | (*pah*-dray/ pah-*pah*) |
| son | *hijo* | (ee-hoh) |
| daughter | *hija* | (ee-hah) |
| cousin (M) | *primo* | (pree-moh) |
| cousin (F) | *prima* | (pree-mah) |
| adult (M) | *adulto* | (ah-*dool*-toh) |
| adult (F) | *adulta* | (ah-*dool*-tah) |
| boss | *jefe* | (heh-fay) |
| friend (M) | *amigo* | (ah-*mee*-goh) |
| friend (F) | *amiga* | (ah-*mee*-gah) |
| boyfriend | *novio* | (noh-vee-oh) |
| girlfriend | *novia* | (noh-vee-ah) |

 If you want to discuss more than one of a noun, add an *-s* to the end. For example, the word for "boys" is *niños* (nee-*nyohs*). There are a few exceptions to this practice, but for the most part, it's the rule.

# Useful Expressions and Phrases

| | | |
|---|---|---|
| Thank you very much. | *Muchas gracias.* | (*mooch*-ahs grah-see-ahs) |
| No, thank you. | *No, gracias.* | (noh grah-see-ahs) |
| Nothing, thanks. | *Nada, gracias.* | (nah-dah, *grah*-see-ahs) |

| I'm sorry. | *Lo siento.* | (loh see-*ehn*-toh) |
| My fault. | *Mi culpa.* | (me *kool*-pah) |
| Excuse me (in the way) | *Con permiso* | (kon pehr-*me*-soh) |
| Excuse me (interrupt) | *Discúlpeme* | (dihs-*kool*-peh-meh) |
| What do you need? | *¿Qué necesita usted?* | (kay neh-seh-*see*-tah oo-*sted*?) |
| I want some batteries. | *Quiero unas baterías.* | (kee-*ehr*-oh oo-*nahs* bah-tehr-*ee*-ahs) |
| Do you speak English? | *¿Habla inglés usted?* | (*ahb*-lah een-*glehs* oo-*sted*?) |
| I speak English. | *Hablo inglés.* | (*ahb*-loh een-*glehs*) |
| Do you speak Spanish? | *¿Habla español usted?* | (*ahb*-lah ehs-pah-*nyol* oo-*sted*?) |
| I speak Spanish. | *Hablo español.* | (*ahb*-loh ehs-pah-*nyol*) |
| I don't understand. | *No entiendo.* | (noh ehn-tee-*ehn*-doh) |
| I don't speak much Spanish. | *No hablo mucho español.* | (noh *ahb*-loh mooch-oh ehs-pah-*nyol*) |
| Can you repeat that, please? | *¿Repete, por favor?* | (*reh*-peh-tay, pohr fah-*vohr*?) |
| I need information, please. | *Necesito información, por favor.* | (neh-seh-*see*-toh en-four-mah-see-*ohn*, pohr fah-*vohr*) |

| I need some help. | *Necesito ayuda.* | (neh-seh-*see*-toh eye-*yoo*-dah) |
| Where are you going? | *¿A dónde va usted?* | (ah *don*-day bah oo-*sted*?) |
| I don't know. | *No sé.* | (noh say) |

## Question Words

| Who? | *¿Quién?* | (kee-*ehn*) |
| What? | *¿Qué?* | (kay) |
| Where? | *¿Dónde?* | (*don*-day) |
| When? | *¿Cuándo?* | (*kwan*-doh) |
| Why? | *¿Por qué?* | (pohr *kay*) |
| How? | *¿Cómo?* | (*koh*-moh) |
| How much? | *¿Cuánto es?* | (*kwan*-toh ehs) |
| How many? | *¿Cuántos son?* | (*kwan*-tohs sohn) |
| Is/Are there? | *¿Hay?* | (eye) |

## Useful Questions (and Answers)

Remember that personal pronouns may be omitted in statements if the subject is clearly implied.

| Who is that man? | *¿Quién es ese hombre?* | (kee-*ehn* ehs ehs-ay *ohm*-bray) |
| He is the driver. | *Es el chofer.* | (ehs ehl choh-*fehr*) |

| What time is it? | ¿Qué hora es? | (*kay* or-ah ehs) |
| It's 1 p.m. | *Es la una p.m.* | (ehs lah *oo*-nah pay-em-may) |
| It's 8 a.m. | *Son las ocho a.m.* | (sohn lahs *oh*-choh ah-em-may) |
| What day is it? | ¿Qué día es? | (*kay* dee-ah ehs) |
| It's Tuesday. | *Es martes.* | (ehs *mahr*-tehs) |
| What is the date? | ¿Qué es la fecha? | (*kay* ehs lah *fay*-chah) |
| It's June 17th. | *Es el diez y siete de junio.* | (ehs ehl dee-*ehz* ee see-*eh*-tay day *hoo*-nee-oh) |
| Where is the supermarket? | ¿Dónde está el supermercado? | (*don*-day ehs-*tah* ehl soo-pehr-mehr-*cah*-doh) |
| It's on Main Street. | *Está en la calle Main.* | (ehs-*tah* ehn lah *kie*-jyay main) |
| When is the meeting? | ¿Cuándo es la junta? | (*kwan*-doh ehs lah *hoon*-tah) |
| At 8 in the morning. | *A las ocho de la mañana.* | (ah lahs *oh*-choh day lah mahn-*yan*-ah) |
| In three days. | *En tres días.* | (ehn trehys *dee*-ahs) |

# _You Can Count on Me: An Overview of Numbers_

| 1 | _uno_ | (oo-noh) |
| 2 | _dos_ | (dohs) |
| 3 | _tres_ | (trehys) |
| 4 | _cuatro_ | (_kwa_-troh) |
| 5 | _cinco_ | (_seen_-koh) |
| 6 | _seis_ | (sehys) |
| 7 | _siete_ | (see-_eh_-tay) |
| 8 | _ocho_ | (_oh_-choh) |
| 9 | _nueve_ | (noo-_ay_-vay) |
| 10 | _diez_ | (dee-_ehz_) |
| 11 | _once_ | (_on_-say) |
| 12 | _doce_ | (_doh_-say) |
| 13 | _trece_ | (_trehy_-say) |
| 14 | _catorce_ | (kah-_tohr_-say) |
| 15 | _quince_ | (_keen_-say) |

To say numbers 16–29, you combine the tens and ones. Instead of using three separate words, you can abbreviate to one word by changing the "z" to a "c" and the "y" to "i." For example, _diez y seis_ becomes _dieciséis_.

| 16 | *dieciséis* | (dee-*ehs*-ee-*sehys*) |
| 17 | *diecisiete* | (dee-*ehs*-ee-see-*eh*-tay) |
| 18 | *dieciocho* | (dee-*ehs*-ee-*oh*-cho) |
| 19 | *diecinueve* | (dee-*ehs*-ee-nooh-*ay*-vay) |
| 20 | *veinte* | (*bayn*-tay) |
| 21 | *veintiuno* | (bayn-tee-*oo*-noh) |
| 22 | *veintidós* | (vayn-tee-*dohs*) |
| 23 | *veintitrés* | (vayn-tee-*treys*) |
| 24 | *veinticuatro* | (bayn-tee-*kwa*-troh) |
| 25 | *veinticinco* | (bayn-tee-*seen*-koh) |
| 26 | *veintiséis* | (bayn-tee-*sehys*) |
| 27 | *veintisiete* | (vayn-tee-see-*eh*-tay) |
| 28 | *veintiocho* | (bayn-tee-*oh*-choh) |
| 29 | *veintinueve* | (bayn-tee-noo-*ay*-vay) |
| 30 | *treinta* | (*trehyn*-tah) |
| 31 | *treinta y uno* | (trehyn-tah ee *oo*-noh) |
| 40 | *cuarenta* | (kwa-*rehn*-tah) |
| 41 | *cuarenta y uno* | (kwa-*rehn*-tah ee *oo*-noh) |
| 50 | *cincuenta* | (seen-*kwen*-tah) |
| 60 | *sesenta* | (say-*sen*-tah) |
| 70 | *setenta* | (say-*ten*-tah) |

| 80 | *ochenta* | (oh-*chen*-tah) |
| 90 | *noventa* | (noh-*ven*-tah) |
| 100 | *cien* | (*see*-en) |
| 101 | *ciento uno* | (*see*-en-toh *oo*-noh) |
| 102 | *ciento dos* | (*see*-en-toh *dohs*) |
| 150 | *ciento cincuenta* | (*see*-en-toh seen-*kwen*-tah) |
| 1,000 | *mil* | (meel) |

## Talking about Time

| time | *la hora* | (lah *or*-ah) |
| hour | *hora* | (*or*-ah) |
| minute | *minuto* | (mih-*noo*-toh) |
| second | *segundo* | (seh-*goon*-doh) |
| morning | *la mañana* | (lah mahn-*yan*-ah) |
| afternoon | *la tarde* | (lah *tahr*-day) |
| night | *la noche* | (lah *noh*-chay) |
| day | *el día* | (ehl *dee*-ah) |
| tomorrow | *mañana* | (mahn-*yan*-ah) |
| yesterday | *ayer* | (eye-*ehr*) |
| today | *hoy* | (oy) |
| What time is it? | *¿Qué hora es?* | (kay *or*-ah ehs?) |

# Going through the Calendar and Forming the Date

## Days

| | | |
|---|---|---|
| Monday | *lunes* | (*loo*-nays) |
| Tuesday | *martes* | (*mahr*-tays) |
| Wednesday | *miércoles* | (me-*ehr*-koh-lays) |
| Thursday | *jueves* | (hoo-*ay*-vays) |
| Friday | *viernes* | (vee-*ehr*-nays) |
| Saturday | *sábado* | (*sah*-bah-doh) |
| Sunday | *domingo* | (doh-*meen*-goh) |

 The words for days and months aren't capitalized in Spanish. Also, the calendar week begins with Monday, unless otherwise stated.

## Months

| | | |
|---|---|---|
| January | *enero* | (eh-*nehr*-oh) |
| February | *febrero* | (feh-*brehr*-oh) |
| March | *marzo* | (*mahr*-soh) |
| April | *abril* | (ahv-*reel*) |
| May | *mayo* | (*my*-oh) |
| June | *junio* | (hoo-*nee*-oh) |
| July | *julio* | (hoo-*lee*-oh) |

| August | *agosto* | (ah-*gohs*-toh) |
| September | *septiembre* | (sep-tee-*ehm*-bray) |
| October | *octubre* | (ok-too-bray) |
| November | *noviembre* | (no-vee-*ehm*-bray) |
| December | *diciembre* | (dee-see-*ehm*-bray) |

## Dates

| February 2nd | *2 de febrero* | (dohs day feh-*brehr*-oh) |
| July 23rd | *23 de julio* | (*vayn*-tee-trehys day *hoo*-lee-oh) |
| November 1st | *el primero de noviembre* | (ehl pree-*mehr*-oh day no-bee-*ehm*-bray) |

When stating the first of any month, it is always *primero* (pree-*mehr*-oh) (first) rather than *el uno* (ehl *oo*-noh) (one). When written numerically, the date may be transposed so that days come before months (such as 23/07 for July 23rd).

# Directions

| to the right | *a la derecha* | (ah lah deh-*ray*-chah) |
| to the left | *a la izquierda* | (ah lah ihs-gee-*ehr*-dah) |
| straight ahead | *todo recto* | (toh-doh *rehk*-toh) |
| to the east | *al este* | (ahl ehs-tay) |
| to the west | *al oeste* | (ahl whes-tay) |

| | | |
|---|---|---|
| to the north | *al norte* | (ahl nohr-tay) |
| to the south | *al sur* | (ahl soohr) |
| next one | *al próximo/ al siguiente* | (ahl *prohx*-ee-moh/ ahl see-gee-*ehn*-tay) |
| next block | *al próximo bloque* | (ahl *prohx*-ee-moh bloh-kay) |
| street | *calle* | (kie-jyay) |
| take | *dé* | (day) |
| up | *arriba* | (ahr-*ree*-bah) |
| down | *abajo* | (ah-*bah*-hoh) |
| through | *por* | (pohr) |
| around | *alrededor* | (ahl-*ray*-day-dohr) |
| next to | *al lado de* | (ahl *lah*-doh day) |

# Chapter 2

# Graduating to Grammar

● ● ● ● ● ● ● ● ● ● ● ● ● ● ● ● ● ● ● ● ● ● ● ● ● ● ● ● ● ● ● ●

*T*his chapter shows you how to use all of the important parts of speech, including nouns, verbs, adjectives, pronouns, and more. And don't forget to try out the simple sentences and questions.

## Singular Nouns and Articles

In Spanish, all nouns (that is, people, places, and things) have a gender. They are either masculine or feminine.

Although there are some exceptions, here's the general rule:

- ✔ If a noun ends in *-o* or *-e,* it's masculine.
- ✔ If a noun ends in *-a,* it's feminine.

The gender of a noun determines which article you use with it. With masculine nouns, you use *un* (oon), to say "a/an", or *el* (ehl) for "the". With feminine nouns, you use *una* (oon-ah) to say "a/an", or *la* (lah) for "the".

## Nouns on the Street

| | | |
|---|---|---|
| country | *un país* | (oon pie-*ees*) |
| city | *una ciudad* | (oon-ah see-yoo-*dad*) |

| | | |
|---|---|---|
| neighborhood | *un vecindario* | (oon veh-seen-*dahr*-ee-oh) |
| bus | *un autobus* | (oon ow-toh-*boos*) |
| taxi | *un taxi* | (oon *tahx*-ee) |
| car | *un coche* | (oon *koh*-chay) |
| train | *un tren* | (oon trehn) |
| station | *una estación* | (oon-ah ehs-tah-see-*ohn*) |
| hotel | *un hotel* | (oon oh-*tehl*) |
| street | *una calle* | (oon-ah *kie*-yay) |
| store | *una tienda* | (oon-ah tee-*ehn*-dah) |
| market | *un mercado* | (oon mehr-*kah*-doh) |
| vendor | *un vendedor* | (oon vehn-day-*dohr*) |
| school | *una escuela* | (oon-ah ehs-*quay*-lah) |
| restaurant | *un restaurante* | (oon rehst-ow-*rahn*-tay) |
| park | *un parque* | (oon *pahr*-kay) |
| office | *una oficina* | (oon-ah off-ee-*see*-nah) |
| house | *una casa* | (oon-ah kah-sah) |
| building | *un edificio* | (oon eh-dee-*fee*-see-oh) |

| library | *una biblioteca* | (oon-ah bib-lee-oh-*teh*-kah) |
| mall | *un centro comercial* | (*oon sehn-troh koh-mehr-see*-ahl) |
| map | *un mapa* | (oon mah-pah) |
| corner | *una esquina* | (oon-ah ehs-*kee*-nah) |
| block | *una cuadra* | (oon-ah kwah-drah) |

## *Nouns for Shopping*

| credit card | *una tarjeta de crédito* | (oon-ah tahr-*heh*-tah day *creh*-dee-toh) |
| dollar | *un dólar* | (oon *doh*-lahr) |
| coin | *una moneda* | (oon-ah moh-nay-dah) |
| discount | *un descuento* | (oon-dehs-koo-*ehn*-toh) |
| price | *un precio* | (oon preh-see-oh) |
| register | *una caja registradora* | (oon-ah kah-hah reh-hees-trah-*dohr*-ah) |
| radio | *una radio* | (oon-ah *rah*-dee-oh) |
| television | *una television* | (oon-ah teh-leh-vih-see-*ohn*) |
| movie | *una película* | (oon-ah peh-*leek*-yoo-lah) |

| toy | *un juguete* | (oon hoo-*geht*-ay) |
| medicine | *una medicina* | (oon-ah meh-dee-*see*-nah) |
| money | *dinero* | (dee-nehr-oh) |
| change | *cambio* | (kahm-bee-oh) |
| music | *música* | (*moo*-see-kah) |
| clothes | *ropa* | (roh-pah) |
| food | *comida* | (oon-ah koh-*mee*-dah) |
| fruit | *fruta* | (froo-*tah*) |
| vegetables | *verduras* | (vehr-duhr-ahs) |
| meat | *carne* | (kahr-nay) |

# Nouns at Home

| house | *una casa* | (oon-ah kah-sah) |
| garage | *un garaje* | (oon gah-*rah*-hay) |
| kitchen | *una cocina* | (oon-ah koh-*see*-nah) |
| dining room | *un comedor* | (oon koh-may-*dohr*) |
| living room | *una sala* | (oon-ah sah-lah) |
| bedroom | *una recámara* | (oon-ah ray-*cahm*-ah-rah) |
| bathroom | *un baño* | (oon bah-nyoh) |
| lawn | *un césped* | (oon *sehs*-pehd) |

| | | |
|---|---|---|
| lamp | *una lámpara* | (oon-ah *lahmp-ahr-ah*) |
| chair | *una silla* | (oon-ah see-yah) |
| sofa | *un sofa* | (oon soh-fah) |
| television | *un televisor* | (oon teh-leh-vee-*sohr*) |
| telephone | *un teléfono* | (oon tehl-*ay*-foh-noh) |
| family | *una familia* | (oon-ah fah-*meel-ee*-ah) |
| man | *un hombre* | (oon ohm-bray) |
| woman | *una mujer* | (oon-ah moo-*hehr*) |
| boy | *un niño* | (oon nee-nyo) |
| girl | *una niña* | (oon-ah nee-nya) |
| brother | *un hermano* | (oon ehr-*mah*-noh) |
| sister | *una hermana* | (oon-ah ehr-*mah*-nah) |

# The Verb Ser (to Be)

You use the verb *ser* (sehr) (to be) with adjectives because the adjectives are physical attributes or qualities that are unchanging or permanent in a thing or person.

| | | |
|---|---|---|
| to be | *ser* | (sehr) |
| I am | *(yo) soy* | (yo soy) |
| you are (S/Informal) | *(tú) eres* | (too ehr-ehs) |

| | | |
|---|---|---|
| you are (S/Formal) | *usted es* | (oos-*sted* ehs) |
| he is | *él es* | (*ehl* ehs) |
| she is | *ella es* | (ay-yah ehs) |
| we are | *nosotros somos* | (noh-*soh*-trohs soh-mohs) |
| you are (P) | *ustedes son* | (oos-*sted*-ehs sohn) |
| they are (M) | *ellos son* | (ay-yohs sohn) |
| they are (F) | *ellas son* | (ay-yahs sohn) |

I place some of the personal pronouns in parentheses because you don't have to use them. However, if you need to make a distinction with "he" or "she," for example, then pronouns are necessary.

# Adjectives

Adjectives physically describe nouns. In Spanish, they also describe nouns in number and gender. You can use the same adjectives for masculine or feminine nouns. Put an -*a* at the end of an adjective paired with a feminine noun or an -*o*, or *consonant,* at the end of an adjective paired with a masculine noun.

Practice paring adjectives with feminine and masculine nouns:

| | | |
|---|---|---|
| The woman is tall. | *La mujer es alta.* | (lah moo-*hehr* ehs ahl-tah) |

| The man is tall. | *El hombre es alto.* | (ehl ohm-bray ehs ahl-toh) |

Add an *-s* to the end of an adjective that describes plural nouns:

| The women are tall. | *Las mujeres son altas.* | (lahs moo-*hehr*-ehs sohn ahl-tahs) |
| The men are tall. | *Los hombres son altos.* | (lohs ohm-brays sohn ahl-tohs) |

 In some cases, the adjective is the same regardless of the gender of the noun it describes.

# Colors (M/F)

| red | *rojo/a* | (roh-hoh/roh-hah) |
| blue | *azul* | (ah-zool) |
| yellow | *amarillo/a* | (ah-mah-*ree*-yoh/ ah-mah-ree-yah) |
| green | *verde* | (*behr*-day) |
| orange | *anaranjado/a* | (ah-nah-rahn-*hah*-doh/ah-nah-rahn-*hah*-dah) |
| purple | *morado/a* | (moh-*rah*-doh/moh-*rah*-dah) |
| brown | *café* | (kah-*fay*) |

| black | *negro/a* | (nay-groh/nay-grah) |
| white | *blanco/a* | (blahn-koh/blahn-kah) |

## *Attributes (M/F)*

| good | *bueno/a* | (*bway*-noh/*bway*-nah) |
| bad | *malo/a* | (mah-loh/mah-lah) |
| important | *importante* | (ihm-pohr-*tahn*-tay) |
| tall | *alto/a* | (ahl-toh/ahl-tah) |
| short | *bajo/a* | (bah-hoh/bah-hah) |
| big | *grande* | (grahn-day) |
| little | *chico/a* | (chee-koh/chee-kah) |
| pretty | *bonito/a* | (boh-*nee*-toh/boh-nee-tah) |
| ugly | *feo/a* | (fay-oh/fay-ah) |
| fast | *rápido/a* | (*rah*-pee-doh/*rah*-pee-dah) |
| slow | *lento/a* | (lehn-toh/lehn-tah) |
| cheap | *barato/a* | (bah-*rah*-toh/bah-*rah*-tah) |
| expensive | *caro/a* | (kah-roh/kalı-rah) |
| easy | *fácil* | (*fah*-seel) |
| difficult | *difícil* | (dee-*fee*-seel) |
| sad | *triste* | (trees-tay) |
| happy | *feliz* | (feh-*lees*) |
| young | *jóven* | (*hoh*-vehn) |

| old | *viejo/a* | (bee-*yay*-hoh/bee-*yay*-hah) |
| cold | *frío/a* | (*free*-yoh/*free*-yah) |
| hot | *caluroso;* *caliente* | (kah-loor-*oh*-soh; kah-lee-*ehn*-tay) |
| open | *abierto/a* | (ah-bee-*ehr*-toh/ ah-bee-*ehr*-tah) |
| closed | *cerrado/a* | (sehr-*rah*-doh/ sehr-*rah*-dah) |
| light | *ligero(a);* *liviano(a)* | (lee-*hehr*-oh/lee-*hehr*-ah); (lih-vee-*ah*-noh/ lih-vee-*ah*-nah) |
| heavy | *pesado/a* | (pay-*sah*-doh/pay-*sah*-dah) |
| weak | *débil* | (*day*-veel) |
| strong | *fuerte* | (foo-*wehr*-tay) |

# *Degrees of Adjectives and Common Comparisons*

When making a comparison using an adjective, the adjective must agree in gender and in number with the noun being described. Changing the *-o* at the end of the adjective to -a indicates that the noun is feminine. Also, adding *-s, -as,* or *-es* (after a consonant) indicates a plural noun.

| a lot | *mucho* | (*mooch*-oh) |
| more | *más* | (*mahs*) |
| a little | *poco* | (poh-koh) |

| less | *menos* | (may-nohs) |
| very | *muy* | (moo-ee) |
| not so | *no tan* | (noh tahn) |
| good | *bueno* | (*bway*-noh) |
| better | *mejor* | (may-*hohr*) |
| best | *el mejor* | (ehl may-*hohr*) |
| bad | *malo* | (mah-loh) |
| worse | *peor* | (pay-ohr) |

Can't remember which comparison word to use? Try adding *muy* (very) and *no tan* (not so) in front of an adjective. For example, *muy alto* is "very tall," (moo-ee ahl-toh) and *no tan alto* is "not so tall" (noh tahn ahl-toh).

## Prepositions

| to | *a* | (ah) |
| at | *a* | (ah) |
| from | *de* | (day) |
| of | *de* | (day) |
| by/through/for | *por* | (pohr) |
| for (intent) | *para* | (pah-rah) |
| behind | *detrás de* | (day-*trahs* day) |
| above | *arriba de* | (ahr-*ree*-bah day) |

| on | *en* | (ehn) |
| under | *debajo de* | (day-*vah*-hoh day) |
| in | *en/dentro de* | (ehn/dehn-troh day) |
| out | *fuera de* | (foo-*wehr*-ah day) |
| around | *alrededor de* | (ahl-ray-day-*dohr* day) |
| here | *aquí* | (ah-*kee*) |
| over here | *acá* | (ah-*kah*) |
| there | *allí* | (ah-*yee*) |

## Conjunctions

| and | *y* | (ee) |
| but | *pero* | (peh-roh) |
| either | *tampoco* | (tahm-*poh*-koh) |
| or | *o* | (oh) |
| yet | *todavía* | (toh-dah-*vee*-yah) |

## Forming Simple Sentences

Crafting a sentence in Spanish is very similar to making one in English. The necessary basics are: a subject (pronoun/noun) + conjugated verb + predicate (a preposition, conjunction, adjective, or object noun). And remember, pronouns aren't always necessary.

| I'm going to my house. | *Yo voy a mi casa.* | (yoh voy ah me kah-sah) |

| The offices are closed. | *Las oficinas están cerradas.* | (lahs off-ee-*seen*-ahs ehs-*tahn* sehr-*rah*-dohs) |
| The sky is dark. | *El cielo es oscuro.* | (ehl see-*ay*-loh ehs os-*kuhr*-roh) |
| You look pretty. | *Tú eres bonita.* | (too ehr-ehs boh-*nee*-tah) |

## Forming Negative Sentences

Changing a sentence to the negative is very simple: Just put *no* in front of the conjugated verb. The tense doesn't matter. Check out these examples of negative sentences.

| I'm not going to my house. | *Yo no voy a mi casa.* | (yoh *noh* voy ah me kah-sah) |
| The offices aren't closed. | *Las oficinas no están cerradas.* | (lahs off-ee-*seen*-ahs *noh* ehs-*tahn* sehr-*rah*-dohs) |

## Forming Questions

You can form a question in one of three ways. The first is by using question words:

- *quién* (who)   (kee-*ehn*)
- *qué* (what)   (*kay*)

| ✔ *dónde* (where) | (*don*-day) |
| ✔ *cuándo* (when) | (*kwan*-doh) |
| ✔ *por qué* (why) | (pohr *kay*) |
| ✔ *cómo* (how) | (*koh*-moh) |

When using question words, the subject pronoun/noun comes at the end. Here are examples:

| Where are you going? | *¿Dónde vas tú?* | (*don*-day vahs *too*?) |
| Why is the meal cold? | *¿Por qué está frío el plato?* | (pohr *kay* ehs-*tah free*-oh ehl plah-toh?) |

You can also ask questions by reversing the subject noun/pronoun and conjugated verb. And saying a regular sentence with the intonation of a question is the third way to ask a question.

38

# Chapter 3

# Chatting It Up at Work and on the Town

● ● ● ● ● ● ● ● ● ● ● ● ● ● ● ● ●

**D**iscover vocabulary for making conversation in the workplace, asking for help or directions, eating out, staying at a hotel, doing business, banking, and shopping.

## *At the Office*
### *Vocabulary*

| | | |
|---|---|---|
| account | *cuenta* | (*kooehn*-tah) |
| coffee | *café* | (kah-*feh*) |
| elevator | *ascensor* | (ah-sehn-*sohr*) |
| e-mail | *correo electrónico* | (koh-*rreh*-oh eh-lehk-*troh*-nee-koh) |
| identification | *identificación* | (ee-dehn-tee-fee-kay-see*ohn*) |
| keyboard | *teclado* | (tehk-*lah*-doh) |
| letter | *carta* | (*kahr*-tah) |
| mail | *correo* | (koh-*rreh*-oh) |

| meeting | *reunión* | (rehoo-nee-*ohn*) |
| newspaper | *diario* | (dee*ah*-reeoh) |

# On the Job
## Vocabulary

| dentist | *dentista* | (dehn-*tees*-tah) |
| doctor | *médico* | (*meh*-dee-koh) |
| engineer | *ingeniero* | (een-heh-nee*eh*-roh) |
| lawyer | *abogado* | (ah-bvoh-*gah*doh) |
| manager | *gerente* | (heh-*rehn*-teh) |
| photographer | *fotógrafo* | (foh-*toh*-grah-foh) |
| pilot | *piloto* | (pee-*loh*-toh) |

For a feminine subject in a role, make the article feminine and change the *–o* to an *–a*, if necessary. If the noun ends with a consonant, add an *–a*. If it ends with an *–e*, don't change it.

# Making Appointments
## Vocabulary

| appointment | *la cita* | (lah *see*-tah) |
| message | *el mensaje* | (ehl mehn-*sah*-hay) |
| time | *la hora* | (lah or-ah) |

| morning | *la mañana* | (lah mahn-*yan*-ah) |
| afternoon | *la tarde* | (lah *tahr*-day) |
| night | *la noche* | (lah *noh*-chay) |
| day | *el día* | (ehl *dee*-ah) |
| phone number | *el número de teléfono* | (ehl *noo*-mehr-oh day tel-*ay*-foh-noh) |
| address | *la dirección* | (lah dee-rehk-see-*ohn*) |

## Verbs

| to meet | *reunir* | (ray-ooh-neer) |
| to be available | *estar disponible* | (ehs-*tahr* dis-pohn-*ee*-blay) |
| to make an appointment | *hacer una cita* | (ah-*sehr* oon-ah *see*-tah) |
| to be busy | *estar ocupado* | (ehs-*tahr* oh-koo-*pah*-doh) |
| to call | *llamar* | *(jyah*-mahr)* |
| to confirm | *verificar* | (behr-if-ee-*kahr*) |

# Making Travel Arrangements
## Vocabulary

| ticket | *el boleto* | (ehl boh-*leh*-toh) |
| reservation | *la reservación* | (lah reh-zehr-vah-see-*ohn*) |

| representative | *el representante* | (ehl reh-pray-zehn-*tahn*-tay) |
| flight | *el vuelo* | (ehl voo-*way*-loh) |
| baggage | *el equipaje* | (ehl eh-kee-*pah*-hay) |
| handbag | *el bolso* | (ehl bohl-so) |
| hotel | *el hotel* | (ehl oh-*tehl*) |
| early | *temprano* | (tehm-*prah*-noh) |
| late | *tarde* | (*tahr*-day) |
| on time | *en punto* | (ehn poon-toh) |
| train | *el tren* | (ehl trehn) |

## Verbs

| I would like | *me gustaría* | (may goos-tahr-*ee*-ah) |
| to pay cash | *pagar en efectivo* | (pah-*gahr* ehn eh-fek-*tee*-voh) |
| to reserve | *reservar* | (ray-zehr-*vahr*) |
| to cancel | *cancelar* | (kahn-sehl-*ahr*) |
| to be interested | *tener interés en* | (ten-*ehr* en-tehr-*es* ehn) |
| to arrive | *llegar* | (jyay-*gahr*) |
| to leave | *partir* | (pahr-*teer*) |
| to pay | *pagar* | (pah-*gahr*) |

## Sentences and phrases

| | | |
|---|---|---|
| I would like to reserve a ticket. | *Me gustaría reservar un boleto.* | (may goos-tahr-*ee*-ah ray-zehr-*vahr* oon boh-*leh*-toh) |
| Can this be a carry-on? | *¿Puedo llevar esta?* | (poo-way-doh jyay-*vahr ehs*-tah?) |

# Asking for Directions
## Vocabulary

| | | |
|---|---|---|
| map | *el mapa* | (ehl mah-pah) |
| district | *el distrito* | (ehl dis-*tree*-toh) |
| town | *el pueblo* | (ehl *pweh*-bloh) |
| city | *la ciudad* | (lah see-yoo-*dad*) |
| downtown | *el centro* | (ehl *sehn*-troh) |
| street | *la calle* | (lah *kie*-yay) |
| corner | *la esquina* | (lah ehs-*kee*-nah) |
| movie theater | *el cine* | (ehl *see*-nay) |
| museum | *el museo* | (ehl moo-*zay*-oh) |
| train station | *la estación de trenes* | (lah ehs-tah-see-*ohn* day *trehy*-nehs) |
| school | *la escuela* | (lah ehs-*kway*-lah) |
| bank | *el banco* | (ehl bahn-koh) |

| church | *la iglesia* | (lah ee-*glay*-see-ah) |
| taxi | *el taxi* | (ehl *tahx*-ee) |
| direction | *la dirección* | (lah dee-rek-see-*ohn*) |
| here | *aquí* | (ah-*kee*) |
| there | *allí* | (ah-*yee*) |
| right | *la derecha* | (lah deh-*ray*-chah) |
| left | *la izquierda* | (lah ihz-gee-*yehr*-dah) |

## *Sentences and phrases*

| May I ask you for directions? | *¿Puedo pedirles indicaciones?* | (poo-way-doh pay-*deer*-lehys ihn-dee-kah-see-*ohn*-ays?) |
| How do I get to the museum? | *¿Cómo voy yo al museo?* | (*koh*-moh voy yoh ahl moo-*zay*-oh?) |
| Where is the nearest bank? | *¿Dónde está el banco más cercano?* | (*don*-day ehs-*stah* ehl bahn-koh *mahs* sehr-*kahn*-oh?) |
| Go straight and you'll find it. | *Vaya derecho y lo encontrará.* | (bie-ah deh-*ray*-choh ee loh en-kon-trahr-*ah*) |

# *Asking for and Getting Help*
## *Vocabulary*

| help | *ayuda* | (eye-*yoo*-dah) |
| health | *la salud* | (lah sah-*lood*) |

| hospital | *el hospital* | (ehl ohs-pee-*tahl*) |
| doctor | *el doctor* | (ehl dok-*tohr*) |
| surgery | *cirugía* | (see-roo-*heeah*) |
| pharmacy | *la farmacia* | (lah far-*mah*-see-ah) |
| prescription | *receta* | (reh-*seh*-tah) |
| aspirin | *la aspirina* | (lah ahs-peer-*een*-ah) |
| pills | *las pastillas* | (lahs pahs-*tee*-yahs) |
| headache | *el dolor de cabeza* | (ehl doh-*lohr* day kah-*bay*-zah) |
| stomachache | *el dolor del estómago* | (ehl doh-*lohr* dehl es-*toh*-mah-goh) |
| cough | *tos* | (tohs) |
| an injury | *la herida* | (lah ehr-*ee*-dah) |
| pain | *la pena* | (lah pay-nah) |
| infection | *la infección* | (lah in-fek-see-*ohn*) |
| fever | *la fiebre* | (lah fee-*ay*-bray) |
| police | *el policía* | (ehl poh-lee-*see*-ah) |
| consulate | *el consulado* | (ehl kon-soo-*lah*-doh) |
| embassy | *la embajada* | (lah em-bah-*ha*-dah) |
| phone number | *el número de teléfono* | (ehl *noo*-mehr-oh day tel-*ay*-foh-noh) |
| passport | *el pasaporte* | (ehl pas-ah-*pohr*-tay) |
| insurance | *el seguro* | (ehl say-gu-roh) |

| | | |
|---|---|---|
| well | *bien* | (vee-*ehn*) |
| bad | *malo* | (mah-loh) |
| terrible | *horrible* | (ohr-*ree*-blay) |
| arm | *brazo* | (*bvrah*-soh) |
| chest | *pecho* | (*peh*-choh) |
| ear | *oreja* | or-*reh*-hah) |
| eye | *ojo* | (*oh*-hoh) |
| finger | *dedo* | (*deh*-doh) |
| foot | *pie* | (pee*eh*) |
| hair | *pelo* | (*peh*-loh) |
| head | *cabeza* | (kah-*bveh*-sah) |
| leg | *pierna* | (pee*ehr*-nah) |
| neck | *cuello* | (koo*eh*-yoh) |
| nose | *nariz* | (nah-*rees)* |
| shoulder | *hombro* | (*ohm*-broh) |
| stomach | *estómago* | (ehs-*toh*-mah-goh) |
| throat | *garganta* | (gahr-*gahn*-tah) |
| toe | *dedo del pie* | (*deh*-doh dehl pee*eh)* |
| tooth | *diente* | (dee*ehn*-teh) |
| blood | *la sangre* | (lah *sahn*-gray) |
| bone | *el hueso* | (ehl oo-*way*-soh) |

| body | *el cuerpo* | (ehl koo-*ehr*-poh) |
| heart | *el corazón* | (ehl kor-ah-*zohn*) |

## Emergency sentences and phrases

| Will you help me? | *¿Me ayudas?* | (may eye-*yoo*-dahs?) |
| Please help! | *¡Ayuda, por favor!* | (eye-*yoo*-dah pohr fah-*vohr!*) |
| What happened? | *¿Qué pasó?* | (*kay* pah-*soh?*) |
| I don't know. | *No sé.* | (noh *say*) |
| I can't breathe. | *No puedo respirar.* | (noh poo-*way*-doh rehs-peer-*ahr*) |
| She needs a doctor. | *Ella necesita un doctor.* | (*ay*-yah neh-seh-*see*-tah oon dok-*tohr*) |
| Where is a phone? | *¿Dónde hay un teléfono?* | (*don*-day eye oon tel-*ay*-foh-noh) |
| Where is a hospital? | *¿Dónde está el hospital?* | (*don*-day ehs-*tah* ehl ohs-pee-*tahl?*) |
| I've just been robbed. | *Alguien me robó.* | (*ahl*-gee-ehn may ro-*boh*) |

# At the Restaurant
## Vocabulary

| restaurant | *el restaurante* | (ehl rest-ow-*rahn*-tay) |
| menu | *el menu* | (ehl meh-*noo*) |

| service | *el servicio* | (ehl sehr-*vee*-see-oh) |
|---|---|---|
| breakfast | *el desayuno* | (ehl deh-sahy-*oon*-oh) |
| lunch | *el almuerzo* | (ehl ahl-moo-*ehr*-zoh) |
| dinner | *la cena* | (lah say-nah) |
| dessert | *el postre* | (ehl *pos*-tray) |
| today's special | *el especial de hoy* | (ehl ehs-peh-see-*al* day oy) |
| silverware | *los cubiertos* | (lohs koo-bee-*ehr*-tohs) |
| table | *la mesa* | (lah *may*-sah) |
| chair | *la silla* | (lah see-yah) |
| refreshments | *los refrescos* | (lohs ray-*frehs*-kohs) |
| water (carbonated) | *el agua gaseoso* | (ehl ah-gwah gah-see-*oh*-soh) |
| coffee | *el café* | (ehl ka-*fay*) |
| milk | *la leche* | (lah *lay*-chay) |
| wine | *vino* | (*bveeh*-noh) |
| meat | *la carne* | (lah *kahr*-nay) |
| pork | *el cerdo* | (ehl *sehr*-doh) |
| chicken | *el pollo* | (ehl poh-yoh) |
| fish | *el pescado* | (ehl pehs-*ka*-doh) |

| eggs | *los huevos* | (lohs hoo-*way*-vohs) |
| vegetables | *los vegetales* | (lohs beh-hay-*tahl*-ays) |
| fruit | *la fruta* | (lah *froo*-tah) |
| ice cream | *el helado* | (ehl ay-*lah*-doh) |
| chocolate | *el chocolate* | (ehl chok-oh-*lah*-tay) |
| cake | *el pastel* | (ehl pahs-*tehl*) |
| bread | *el pan* | (ehl pahn) |
| cold | *frío* | (*free*-oh) |
| hot | *caliente* | (kahl-ee-*ehn*-tay) |
| server | *el mesero* | (ehl may-*sehr*-oh) |
| bill | *la cuenta* | (lah *kwen*-tah) |
| tip | *la propina* | (lah proh-*pee*-nah) |

## Verbs

| I would like | *me gustaría* | (may goos-tahr-*ee*-ah) |
| to order | *ordenar* | (or-dehn-*ahr*) |

## Sentences and phrases

| I would like some water, please. | *Me gustaría un agua, por favor.* | (may goos-tahr-*ee*-ah oon ah-gwah, pohr fah-*vohr*) |

| What is today's special? | ¿Qué es el especial de hoy? | (*kay* ehs ehl ehs-peh-see-*ahl* day oy?) |
| Do you serve soup? | ¿Se sirve la sopa? | (say *seer*-vay lah soh-pah?) |

# At the Hotel

## Vocabulary

| hotel | el hotel | (ehl oh-*tehl*) |
| room | una habitación | (oon-*ah* ah-bih-tah-see-*ohn*) |
| key | la llave | (lah *jyah*-vay) |
| bed | la cama | (lah kah-mah) |
| sheets | las sábanas | (lahs *sah*-vah-nahs) |
| pillow | la almohada | (lah ahl-mo-*ha*-dah) |
| single room | una habitación individual | (oon-*ah* ah-bih-tah-see-*ohn* in-dee-vid-oo-*ahl*) |
| reservation | la reservación | (lah reh-sehr-vah-see-*ohn*) |
| date | la fecha | (lah *fay*-chah) |
| check-in time | hora de llegada | (or-ah day jyay-*gah*-dah) |
| check-out time | hora de salida | (or-ah day sah-*lee*-dah) |

| bill | *la cuenta* | (lah *kwen*-tah) |
| payment | *el pago* | (ehl *pah*-goh) |
| air conditioning | *aire acondicionado* | (*eye*-ray ah-kon-dih-see-oh-*nah*-doh) |
| elevator | *el elevador* | (ehl ehl-ay-bah-*dohr*) |
| stairs | *las escaleras* | (lahs es-kah-*lehr*-ahs) |
| room service | *el servicio de habitación* | (ehl sehr-*vee*-see-oh day ah-bih-tah-see-*ohn*) |
| bathroom | *el baño* | (ehl bah-nyoh) |
| toilet | *el utilisario* | (ehl oo-til-ee-*sahr*-ee-oh) |

## Verbs

| to rent | *rentar* | (rehn-*tahr*) |
| to reserve | *reservar* | (ray-sehr-*vahr*) |
| to cancel | *cancelar* | (kahn-sehl-*ahr*) |

## Sentences and phrases

| Are there rooms available? | *¿Hay cuartos disponibles?* | (eye *kwahr*-tohs dihs-poh-*nee*-blays?) |
| I'd like a single bed. | *Me gustaría una cama individual.* | (may goos-tahr-ee-*ah* oon-*ah* kah-mah in-dee-vid-oo-*ahl*) |

# At the Bank

## Vocabulary

| | | |
|---|---|---|
| bank | *el banco* | (ehl *bahn*-koh) |
| money | *el dinero* | (ehl dee-*nehr*-oh) |
| bills | *los billetes* | (lohs bee-*yet*-ays) |
| change | *el cambio* | (ehl *kahm*-bee-oh) |
| account | *la cuenta* | (lah *kwen*-tah) |
| checking | *cuenta de cheques* | (*kwen*-tah day *cheh*-kays) |
| exchange rate | *el precio de intercambio* | (ehl *preh*-see-oh day in-tehr-*kahm*-bee-oh) |
| traveler's checks | *los cheques viajeros* | (lohs *cheh*-kays bee-ah-*hehr*-ohs) |
| country | *el país* | (ehl pie-*ees*) |
| cashier | *la cajera* | (lah kah-*hehr*-ah) |
| safe | *la caja de seguridad* | (lah kah-hah day say-gu-ree-*dahd*) |
| signature | *la firma* | (lah *feer*-mah) |

## Verbs

| | | |
|---|---|---|
| to change | *cambiar* | (kahm-bee-*ahr*) |
| to verify | *verificar* | (vehr-if-ee-*kahr*) |
| to buy | *comprar* | (kom-*prahr*) |

| to make change | *hacer cambio* | (ah-*sehr kahm*-bee-oh) |
| to sign | *firmar* | (feer-*mahr*) |
| to wait | *esperar* | (ehs-pehr-*ahr*) |

## Sentences and phrases

| What is the exchange rate today? | *¿Cuál es la tasa de cambio hoy?* | (*kwal* ehs lah tah-sah day *kahm*-bee-oh oy?) |
| Today's exchange rate is . . . | *El precio de hoy es . . .* | (ehl *preh*-see-oh day oy ehs) |
| I would like to exchange $100. | *Me gustaría cambiar cien dólares.* | (may goos-tahr-*ee*-ah kahm-bee-*ahr* see-*ehn doh*-lahr-ays) |
| Here is my identification. | *Aquí está mi identificación.* | (ah-*kee* ehs-*tah* me ee-dehn-tee-fee-kah-see-*ohn*) |

# At the Store

## Vocabulary

| store | *la tienda* | (lah tee-*ehn*-dah) |
| market | *el mercado* | (ehl mehr-*kah*-doh) |
| mall | *el centro comercial* | (ehl *sehn*-troh koh-mehr-see-*ahl*) |
| supermarket | *el supermercado* | (ehl soo-pehr-mehr-*kah*-doh) |

| cheap | *barato* | (bah-*rah*-toh) |
| expensive | *caro* | (*kah*-roh) |
| sale | *venta* | (*behn*-tah) |
| discount | *el descuento* | (ehl dehs-*kwen*-toh) |
| price | *precio* | (*preh*-seeoh) |
| open | *abierto* | (ah-bee-*ehr*-toh) |
| closed | *cerrado* | (sehr-*rah*-doh) |
| entrance | *la entrada* | (lah ehn-*trah*-dah) |
| exit | *la salida* | (lah sah-*lee*-dah) |
| parking | *estacionamiento* | (ehs-tah-seeoh-nah-mee-*ehn*-toh) |
| size | *el tamaño* | (ehl tah-*mah*-nyoh) |
| small | *chico* | (*chee*-koh) |
| medium | *mediano* | (may-dee-*ah*-noh) |
| large | *grande* | (*grahn*-day) |
| extra large | *extra grande* | (*ayx*-trah *grahn*-day) |
| clothing | *la ropa* | (lah *roh*-pah) |
| hygiene products | *los productos de higiene personal* | (lohs proh-*dook*-tohs day ee-jee-*ehn*) |
| jewelry | *la joyería* | (lah hoy-ehr-*ee*-ah) |
| furniture | *mueble* | (moo*eh*-bvleh) |

| | | |
|---|---|---|
| department | *departamento* | (day-pahr-tah-*men*-toh) |
| receipt | *el recibo* | (ehl ray-*see*-voh) |
| cash | *en efectivo* | (ehn ee-fehk-*tee*-vo) |
| credit card | *la tarjeta de crédito* | (lah tahr-*heh*-tah day *kreh*-dee-toh) |

## Verbs

| | | |
|---|---|---|
| to buy | *comprar* | (kom-*prahr*) |
| to cost | *costar* | (kohs-*tahr*) |
| to pay | *pagar* | (pah-*gahr*) |
| to think about | *pensar en* | (pehn-*sahr* ehn) |
| to return | *regresar* | (ray-greh-*sahr*) |

## Sentences and phrases

| | | |
|---|---|---|
| How many? | *¿Cuántos hay?* | (*kwan*-tohs *eye*?) |
| I like that one. | *Me gusta eso.* | (may *goos*-tah ehs-oh) |
| Are there more? | *¿Hay más?* | (eye *mahs*?) |
| Does your store sell . . . ? | *¿Se vende . . . ?* | (say *behn*-day?) |
| How much is this shirt? | *¿Cuánto cuesta esta camisa?* | (*kwan*-toh *kwehs*-tah *ehs*-tah kah-*mee*-sah?) |

| It's $11.50. | *Cuesta once dólares y cincuenta centavos.* | (*kwehs*-tah *on*-say *doh*-lahr-ays ee seen-*kwen*-tah sen-*tah*-vohs) |
| Do you have this in size small? | *¿Tiene esto de tamaño chico?* | (tee-*ehn*-ay *ehs*-toh day tah-*mah*-nyoh *chee*-koh?) |
| How much does it cost? | *¿Cuánto cuesta?* | (*kwan*-toh *kwes*-tah?) |

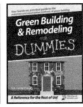